GROWING VEGETABLES in STRAW BALES

Easy Planting, Less Weeding, Early Harvests

Craig LeHoullier

Storey Publishing

*The mission of Storey Publishing is to serve our customers by
publishing practical information that encourages
personal independence in harmony with the environment.*

Edited by Corey Cusson and Carleen Madigan
Series design by Alethea Morrison
Art direction by Jeff Stiefel
Text production by Theresa Wiscovitch
Indexed by Nancy D. Wood

Cover illustration by © Lisel Ashlock
Interior illustrations by © Michael Gellatly

Storey Publishing
210 MASS MoCA Way
North Adams, MA 01247
www.storey.com

Printed in the United States by McNaughton & Gunn, Inc.
10 9 8 7 6 5 4 3 2 1

Library of Congress Cataloging-in-Publication Data
LeHoullier, Craig, author.
  Growing vegetables in straw bales : easy planting, less weeding, early harvests /
by Craig LeHoullier.
      pages cm
  Includes bibliographical references and index.
  ISBN 978-1-61212-614-2 (pbk. : alk. paper)
  ISBN 978-1-61212-615-9 (ebook) 1. Vegetables—Artificial growing media. 2.
  Straw—Utilization. 3. Plant growing media, Artificial. I. Title.
  SB321.L38 2015
  635—dc23
                                    2015034738

CONTENTS

Dedicated to my dad,
Wilfred ("Wild Fred") LeHoullier,
who would have gotten such a kick out of this!

ACKNOWLEDGMENTS

My love of gardening was instilled in me as a very young child, as I spent hours in the garden with my dad, Wilfred, and grandfather, Walter. The tendency to think of my own eventual gardens as projects — essentially my laboratories — grew during my years in college under the guidance of wonderful professors such as Ken Borst, John Williams, Gordon Gribble, and Charles Marzzarcco. All of my gardening adventures were encouraged by my wife, Susan, and daughters Sara and Caitlin. A fascination with gardening using straw bales grew from a chance meeting with Kent Rogers, when "NC Tomatoman" met "NC Straw Bale Man." I was sold from that first exciting discussion, gave it a thorough first try in 2014, and the result is this book. Thanks also to Carleen and Corey at Storey Publishing for helping me turn my fascination with straw bales into something that I can share with others.

INTRODUCTION

Most people think of bales of straw as Halloween or other autumn decorations. Some people use straw bales as building material for temporary or permanent structures. Gardeners frequently use straw as an effective mulch to hold in moisture and prevent weed growth. It may come as a surprise, however, to learn that straw bales are perfect plant hosts for successful gardens.

I first heard about growing plants in straw bales from my gardening friend Kent Rogers, whom many gardeners consider to be an expert in the technique. Kent is extremely enthusiastic about it, and what he described sounded too good to be true: a gardening technique that's simple, flexible, effective, and relatively inexpensive. It was also something new and different to me, making it a perfect project for me to tackle as I learned more about gardening. Along with providing healthy food and good exercise, gardening should be interesting and enjoyable. I strive to try something new each season, and plunging into straw bale gardening sounded like a perfect fit.

My initial experience with straw bale gardening was just wonderful. I grew many types of tomatoes, peppers, eggplant, squash, and cucumbers in the nearly 20 bales that were sprinkled throughout my main garden and driveway growing areas. As an avid container gardener, I appreciated a reduction in the need to fill large pots with expensive potting mix. With the various heirloom tomatoes I chose for the bales, having a disease-free start to seedlings translated to better results when compared to growing them in my garden soil. Things went so well that I plan to at least double the number of bales for this year's garden. The bales will serve for planting leeks, potatoes, sweet potatoes, and carrots, all of which are a challenge for my soil type but should thrive in the more suitable environment provided by the straw.

TWO TOMATO PLANTS per bale is ideal.

CHAPTER ONE

GETTING STARTED

There's no getting around the fact that gardening is physical work. Although the effort pays off handsomely in fresh, delicious produce, it comes with the unavoidable downsides of a sore back and sweaty clothes. Whether you are turning over the soil in a traditional garden or lugging bags of planting medium for a container garden, you will find it no wonder that gardening is considered good exercise. Happily, straw bale gardening eliminates many of the less enjoyable parts of spring garden preparation. Digging and filling are replaced by simply locating the bales and getting them ready to plant. If that isn't a ringing endorsement of a gardening method, I don't know what is!

HOW IT WORKS

HERE'S THE SIMPLE CONCEPT of straw bale gardening: the straw in a bale breaks down over the course of the garden season to provide an effective "home" for the roots of the plants growing in them.

A bale of straw is like a clean, blank slate. It may be mostly free of plant nutrients, but it is also free of diseases. It acts like a sponge, absorbing water and awaiting application of materials that help the straw break down and produce a perfect environment for the roots.

Although some straw bale gardeners report good results by preparing their bales naturally by simply watering them (see page 31), my own experience with that method was not

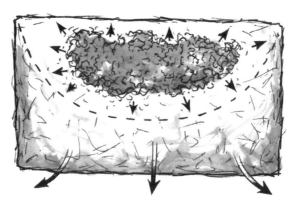

AS YOU WATER AND FERTILIZE the bale, microbial activity generates heat that moves through the bale and breaks down the straw to provide an ideal habitat for plant roots.

as successful. The other basic preparation I recommend consists of regular top additions of high-nitrogen plant food, followed by deep soaking with water. As the straw begins to break down, the process (called *bale cooking*) generates heat and forms an increasingly absorptive structure that supports healthy root growth. Regular watering and feeding, along with the presence of naturally occurring micronutrients, leads to healthy and vigorous plant growth and high yields of produce.

THE BENEFITS

STRAW BALE GARDENING OFFERS several advantages over gardening in the ground or in containers:

- You do not need to dig up soil or fill containers.
- The open structure of the bales provides great drainage, so it's difficult to overwater your plants, even in periods of heavy rain.
- The extra elevation of the plant surface lessens your need to bend as you tend and harvest the plants, and may reduce access to some ground-prowling critters.
- You can position your bales in the part of your property that receives the best sun exposure.

Both conventional and organic gardeners can use the technique, with just a few minor variations in bale treatments. Straw bales are a great option for gardeners whose plants have been seriously affected by soil-borne diseases in the past. Spent bales, at the end of the season, consist of great material to work into your traditional garden beds to loosen the structure.

WHAT'S NOT TO LIKE?

NO SINGLE GARDENING APPROACH or technique is perfect, and each — be it traditional in-ground gardens, raised beds, containers, or straw bales — has strengths, weaknesses, and particular challenges. Here are some considerations specific to straw bale gardening:

- The availability and cost of straw bales can vary widely depending on location.
- It may not be easy to confirm that the bales available to you are herbicide-free, and organic gardeners may have concerns about how the straw was grown.
- For optimum success, you have to allow sufficient time to prepare your bales before planting.
- Feeding and watering schedules are critical, particularly during heat waves and as the plants become large and vigorous.

As a bale absorbs water and is colonized by various decomposing organisms, the straw slowly breaks down to provide even more absorbent material at the plant root zone — forming the perfect environment for root crops like potatoes, beets, and carrots. Straw provides lots of structure but little nutritional value to the plant, so timely feeding is important for vigorous growth.

CHAPTER TWO

GATHERING YOUR MATERIALS

The checklist of essential materials for growing plants in straw bales is quite brief: the bales, some fertilizer (a high-nitrogen fertilizer and a balanced all-purpose fertilizer), and a planting medium. You will also need an inexpensive digital thermometer, especially for the first time you try the method. Throw in some seeds, sun, water, and a trellis or two, and you're good to go.

SELECTING STRAW BALES

STRAW IS SIMPLY THE REMNANT of grain crops, after the heads of grain have been removed. The stems are hollow, allowing good absorption of water into the bale (especially if the bale has been oriented with the hollow ends of the straw facing up).

Straw bales are distinct from hay bales, which comprise various forage grasses and include the seed heads as well as the stems. You can grow plants in hay bales, which provide more of a nutritional boost to the plants as they break down, but they often have far more embedded seeds, leading to significant sprouting on the outside of the bales. (Because straw bales are typically harvested after the seed heads are removed, fewer rogue grass seeds sprout throughout the season.) Also, hay bales are not as structurally solid as straw bales and may therefore break down and sag much more quickly.

Straw Bale Types

Before you start looking for a good source, it's important to select the type of straw bale that will work best for your garden.

The types you can choose from will be determined by the region in which you live. Most commercially available straw bales are composed of wheat straw. Oats, rye, barley, and alfalfa also work well for gardening, but bales made up of these types of straw are less commonly available in most places. My suggestion is to either do some research online, such as perusing local Craigslist or newspaper classified ads, or call your local garden centers, farm supply stores, or hardware stores that carry farm and garden supplies. Be sure to confirm that the bales are pesticide-free, in addition to the type of straw.

It is important to avoid using pine straw bales. Pine needles shed water rather than absorb it, break down very slowly, and tend to be acidic. None of these factors will lead to very happy or productive plants.

Straw Bale Sources

You may be surprised by how many sources there are for straw bales. Garden centers may be the first source you think of, but many big-box stores carry straw bales, too. Be sure to call first; I found that even with a specific chain, availability was very different store to store. An even better source, though, is a local farm. To find a farm source, I recommend searching the local Craigslist or newspaper classified ads, starting in the fall, just after harvest is complete.

Whatever source you choose, be aware that straw bales may contain herbicides. Be sure to ask your bale supplier about this. If you are strictly organic, you will need to be choosy about sourcing organically grown straw bales.

Pricing will vary widely according to where you live and what type of straw you want. Also keep in mind that straw bales are quite heavy and large. If you are planning to use significant numbers, seek to have them delivered to you and factor in the delivery cost as you think about prices. If prices seem prohibitive, perhaps other gardeners nearby would like to grow in straw bales, and you can share the delivery cost.

COMMON BALE MATERIALS

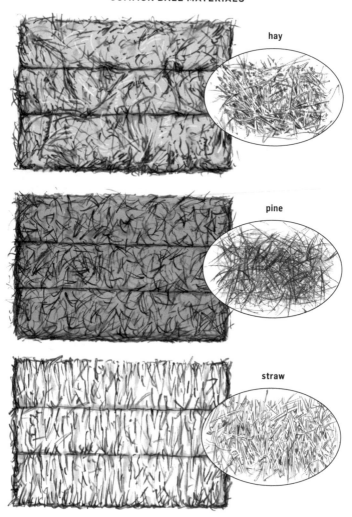

hay

pine

straw

FERTILIZERS

TWO TYPES OF FERTILIZER ARE REQUIRED for straw bale gardening: a high-nitrogen fertilizer to condition the bale, and a balanced fertilizer prior to planting.

Nitrogen is the crucial element in preparing the bale for planting; it speeds the breakdown of the straw to create a good growing environment for the plants. When you check the numbers on fertilizer bags (see page 25), look for a fertilizer with a high first number, which indicates a high amount of nitrogen. For example, many lawn fertilizers are 29-0-4; the high nitrogen content (29 percent) is fine for conditioning your bales.

....

N-P-K

Fertilizers are labeled with three numbers that indicate the relative weight and percentage of the three major nutrients required for healthy plant growth: nitrogen (N), phosphorus (P), and potassium (K). The numbers, referred to as the NPK ratio, are always given in the same order: N-P-K. For example, a bag of fertilizer that is labeled "5-5-5" contains 5 percent nitrogen, 5 percent of phosphorus, and 5 percent of potassium by weight. (The remaining 85 percent is made up of other nutrients and fillers; the fillers allow the nutrients to be spread evenly over a given area.) Products labeled "1-1-1" have 1 percent of each of the three nutrients. It is therefore necessary to use 5 cups of 1-1-1 to equal the feeding power of 1 cup of 5-5-5.

....

Prior to planting in the bales you will also need a balanced plant food with equal quantities of nitrogen (N), phosphorus (P), and potassium (K). The balance will provide the nutrients needed for healthy plants and high production. Look for a product with roughly proportional numbers, such as 5-5-5. You will continue applying the balanced food throughout the growing season.

Straw bale gardening works equally well using chemical or organic fertilizers. Chapter 4 gives details about what kinds to buy and how much to use, but following are some of the basic considerations for each.

Chemical Options

As noted above, high-nitrogen lawn fertilizers are fine for straw bale gardening. Besides lawn fertilizers, other high-nitrogen options are urea, ammonium nitrate, and ammonium sulfate. However, when selecting a high-nitrogen chemical fertilizer, be sure *not* to choose one that is labeled "slow release"; in straw bale gardening the idea is to give the bales a big initial nitrogen kick to get the insides cooking quickly. Also note: *It is critical that the product you purchase not contain herbicides.* (Many lawn fertilizers do.)

Following the initial high-nitrogen treatment, any inexpensive balanced fertilizer can be used.

Organic Options

Organic high-nitrogen fertilizers include heat-dried microbes, blood meal, and fish emulsion, to name just a few. (See page 29 for a list of options.) Since the amount of available nitrogen is lower in these versus traditional treatments (in percent of available nitrogen per volume or weight of the material), more needs to be applied.

As for balanced fertilizers, there are plenty of organic products on the market; again, just look for an NPK ratio as close to 1-1-1 as possible.

PLANTING MEDIUM

ONCE YOUR STRAW BALES ARE FERTILIZED and ready for planting, you'll need a high-quality soilless mix, with some compost or well-aged manure mixed in to improve moisture retention. You will use this to fill in around the planting holes of pre-started seedlings so that you can anchor the plants and provide some moisture retention early on as the root system develops. If you'll be direct-seeding onto the bales, you'll need to apply a layer of the mix (several inches thick) to the top of the bale. This will provide the seeds with enough moisture to germinate and sustain small roots until they grow long enough to penetrate into the bale.

I recommend avoiding commercial bagged potting soil and using a soilless mix instead. Potting soil is often quite heavy and crusts easily, possibly reducing germination when the bales are direct-seeded.

For organic gardeners, it is important to be aware that many commercial soilless mixes contain traces of chemical fertilizer. If this concerns you, either prepare your own planting medium from materials such as peat moss, fine shredded bark, perlite, or vermiculite, and add some of your own compost. You can also select from among the ever-increasing array of organic planting media at a local garden center.

THERMOMETER

PURCHASE AN INEXPENSIVE, rapid-read digital thermometer (typically found in the grilling section of hardware stores) that has a probe of at least 6 inches long. Taking daily temperature readings of your straw bales during the preparation phase will assure you that the internal structure of the bale is breaking down appropriately, which is signaled by a spike in internal temperature. For the first time straw bale gardener, rising temperatures assure that the preparation is working, while falling temperatures confirm that planting time is near. (See chapter 4 for the optimal temperatures.) It's important to avoid planting into bales when the centers are really cooking, as damage to the roots could result. Once you've become familiar with the effect of the treatments on temperature and timing, the need to take temperature measurements becomes more a matter of interest, not necessity.

CHAPTER THREE

PLANNING FOR SUCCESS

All kinds of gardens benefit from good up-front planning, and straw bale gardens are no different. In particular, it's important to plan enough time to prepare the bales before planting, and to ensure consistent watering. Maintaining a notebook or other type of log is helpful; include lists of needed materials, costs, estimated and actual dates for each part of the process, and observations throughout the season. You will have something to reflect back upon at the end of the journey, and a basis for improvements in the next season.

SELECT THE BEST SPOT

WHETHER THEY'RE GROWN in straw bales, in containers, or in the ground, all plants have two basic requirements: sunlight and water. Fortunately, growing vegetables in straw bales allows you a good deal of flexibility. You can place your garden wherever the sun exposure is best, and you can locate the bales so that they're convenient to water. Whether you're watering the bales by hand or with a soaker hose, having easy access to a water spigot will save you time and energy.

Finally, enjoy the freedom from digging holes and avoiding rocky areas. Get out your pencil and paper, and get whimsical with your garden design. Be creative with plant supports. Make a tomato arbor to walk through! Fun, eye-catching straw bale gardens can be a true reflection of your imaginative nature.

Choose the Right Surface

For plants that require staking or trellising, the placement of your straw bale garden will affect the types of supports you can use. If your bale garden is centered on a driveway or patio, you won't be able to drive tall support stakes into the ground; for plants that must be supported, place the bales at the edge of the paved area so that you can drive the supports into the lawn or other piece of unpaved ground. On a deck, you can lash plant stakes to the vertical railing slats; in a yard, you can use fences for support in a similar way.

If you'll be placing the bales on a hard, porous, or absorbent surface such as a wooden deck, consider the effect of constant wetness on that surface. The heavy initial fertilizer treatments, continuous throughout-the-season feeding, and regular watering produces a dark, nutrient-rich runoff that may stain some surfaces. I found that the dark stains washed easily off my concrete driveway, but you may want to consider placing some sort of barrier beneath the bales to protect the surface.

Setting your bales on a flat surface will make them less likely to tilt or tip when the top growth becomes lush and heavy. If the best growing area in your yard is on a slope, you will have to anchor the bales with stakes. Fortunately, though, straw bale gardens on sloped sites are unlikely to experience the kind of soil erosion and washout of young plants and seeds

....

Nobody Likes Weeding

To prevent weeds from growing between and around bales, place your bales on any of the following:

- Hard nonsoil surfaces (wooden deck, concrete or asphalt driveway or patio)
- Landsape fabric (or weed cloth)
- Newspapers
- Mulch (loose straw, untreated grass clippings, sheets of plastic)

One option is to cover your garden plot with landscape fabric and position your bales on top. Weeds won't grow between the bales, and any vining plants will have a suitable surface on which to grow.

....

you might see in a typical in-ground garden after a heavy rainfall. Staking is a small price to pay for the ability to utilize a site that you might not otherwise be able to garden on.

Consider using straw bales in a tired garden spot where the soil is nearly spent from years of use. At the end of the season, you can work the structurally broken-down bales into the garden bed, improving the soil structure, adding nutrients, and thereby revitalizing a useful location.

Consider Your Neighbors

Straw bale gardens look like, well, straw bales with plants growing out of them! As the season progresses and the material within each bale continues to decompose, the bale slowly collapses. By the end of the season, it may look like a graying, irregular clump of dead grasses with plants emerging from the top. It's certainly natural, but not necessarily tidy. If tidiness matters to you or your neighbors, and especially if you live in an area where the appearance of your garden is subject to local regulations (such as homeowners association guidelines), you may want to consider siting your bale garden in location that's not in plain sight. Also keep in mind that with straw bales, your garden is nearly two feet off the ground; the added height may make the garden much more visible than an in-ground garden would be.

Another option to make your straw bale garden more visually appealing is to fashion wooden "holders" for the bales. With this option you are, in essence, creating raised beds that are simply filled with straw bales rather than planting mix.

Though making wooden bale holders requires more work and a higher initial cost, the benefits are twofold: First, volume for volume, a straw bale will be less costly than a commercial planting medium. Second, having bale holders facilitates gardening on significantly sloped areas where freestanding bales would sit at too great an angle to remain upright throughout the season. If the aesthetics of naked bales don't fit into your neighborhood, this is a good solution. With the cost and work involved, however, it is wise to try bale gardening in wooden holders on a small scale first to see if the technique and location work for you.

Plan the Layout

You can work straw bales into your general garden plan. Create a mix of bales interspersed with in-ground or container plants, or place the bales anywhere you wish to have herbs, flowers, or vegetables in areas that have good sun but no existing garden. Plant all of the bales with a single crop, or design a stand-alone mixed garden, in which one bale contains a variety of herbs, a mix of leeks and onions, or tomatoes with basil.

You can stagger the bales by orienting some to sit taller and placing them adjacent to those set shorter; this provides a "table" of bales for vining crops to cascade down to. You can also stack bales to go easy on your back (especially when you're growing short plants) or mass them against one another to create wider growing surfaces.

Arrangement. You can place your bales in geometric arrangements such as semicircles, circles, or L or U shapes.

Let your creativity and imagination be your guide. Whatever configuration you choose, though, be sure to keep in mind the nature of the plants — whether they sprawl or climb, stay compact, or require vertical support. Also ensure that sun-loving plants are not being shaded by taller plants or by surrounding structures (such as fences or buildings) and that shade-loving plants are protected from the sun.

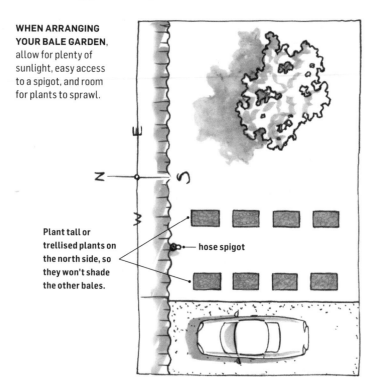

WHEN ARRANGING YOUR BALE GARDEN, allow for plenty of sunlight, easy access to a spigot, and room for plants to sprawl.

Plant tall or trellised plants on the north side, so they won't shade the other bales.

hose spigot

Access. If you're growing plants that will try to spread from the bale onto the ground, such as cucumbers or melons, consider spacing the bales far apart to give yourself enough room to work throughout the season. Some sort of mulch is recommended to keep garden soil from contacting the foliage of the vining plants, to minimize disease. Also bear in mind that if you have lawn between the bales, it will need mowing, which will become complicated if the area is covered with vines.

How many bales will you need? Once you have decided which crops you are most likely to grow in straw bales, refer to chapter 6 for detailed information on each one, along with corresponding recommended plant density. The density recommendations will help you decide how many bales to set up.

TIMING

WHEN DEVISING YOUR BALE GARDEN PLAN, the timing will depend on what you want to grow and how you want to prepare. If you choose the standard bale preparation method — applying heavy doses of nitrogen, alternated with watering (see page 26) — the typical time between bale purchase/placement and planting into the bale is roughly two weeks. If you choose to forgo this step and let the bales become ready naturally with no nutritional additives (see page 31), the preparation time will typically extend to one month.

Temperature and level of direct sun exposure are important factors that will affect prep times. Warmer air and more sun will lead to faster action of the nitrogen fertilizer and possibly reduce the bale preparation time. If you are in an area with a shorter growing season and have cool springs, you can expect a longer prep time. Recording the internal temperature of a bale (see page 26) is helpful in determining when it is ready for planting.

SEEDS OR SEEDLINGS?

WHEN SKETCHING OUT THE PLAN for your straw bale garden, the final key element is determining what you will plant and when. Some crops can be planted directly as seeds, others by settling seedlings into the prepared bales. Chapter 6 discusses the question of whether to direct-sow seeds or transplant seedlings.

When to plant is most often determined by the ambient air temperature, the key parameter being freedom from any further frosts. In this determination, the only difference between other types of gardening and straw bale gardening is knowing when the bales are ready. If you start your own seedlings indoors, you can sync the seed-starting date with your bale preparation schedule.

Bale Orientation

Straw bales can be positioned two ways: strings on top, or strings on the side. There are various rationales for one orientation or the other.

Placing the bales so that the strings are on the side gives you less planting surface but provides a taller bale. It also removes the possibility of inadvertently cutting into the baling twine as you plant, which would lead to collapse of the bale. There are two other things to consider with this orientation: First, with the center of the straw facing upward, water and nutrients can flow more freely through the structure, which may create a slightly greater need for vigilance to ensure adequate plant hydration. Second, the extra height of the bale means tall-growing plants get a bit of a boost but may then require slightly taller plant supports.

If instead you want to orient the bales with the string side up, be careful not to cut the strings when digging into the bale as you prepare to plant your seedlings.

In truth, however, the differences in orientation are so minor that the bale garden will perform equally well no matter which you choose.

strings on top

strings on the side

CHAPTER FOUR

PREPARING THE BALES

Your straw bales are in place. You made all of the necessary decisions about placement, arrangement, surface protection (if needed), and orientation (strings on the top or strings on the side). You have decided what vegetables you want and have either started seeds indoors or planned to purchase seeds or seedlings for the bales. Now you will choose whether to use the standard bale treatment, adding either non-organic or organic nutrients (see next page), or to allow the bales to get ready to plant on their own without any treatment (see page 31). You are almost ready — let's start your straw bale garden.

SELECT A FERTILIZER

As noted in chapter 2, standard (chemical) fertilizers and organic fertilizers work equally well. The decision between them is up to your personal choice. Just remember that the nutrient content of chemical fertilizer tends to be higher by weight, so you can use smaller quantities of it compared with organic fertilizer.

For non-organic growers, a common option carried at most garden centers is high-nitrogen lawn starter with a nitrogen-phosphorous-potassium (NPK) ratio of 29-0-4. Organic growers should initially seek blood meal, which has an NPK ratio of 12-0-0.

In addition to the high-nitrogen fertilizer, non-organic gardeners should purchase a balanced granular product rated 10-10-10. Organic growers should seek out a balanced organic option, such as product rated 3-4-4.

Note that for both the high-nitrogen and balanced additives, there are numerous options, listed on pages 29–30. Whatever option you choose, I recommend using a notebook to record the nutrient addition schedule and temperature data.

PREPARING BALES WITH CHEMICAL FERTILIZERS

Day 1: Check and record the internal temperature of the bale; it will likely be around 80°F. Add ½ cup of the 29-0-4 granular fertilizer, sprinkling it evenly over the top of the bale. Using a hose with no connector and a moderate water flow, add water evenly over the top of the bale for about one minute; you will see water emerging from the bottom of the bale. Note that the water will not visibly dissolve the granular material but will begin to push the material down into the structure of the bale.

Day 2: Check and record the internal temperature of the bale. Water the bale thoroughly from the top.

Day 3: Repeat the Day 1 activity. At this point, you should see the internal bale temperature begin to rise. The temperature should peak at approximately 120°F, which indicates the action of the nutrients on the bale components, breaking them

IT IS EASY TO CHECK the internal temperature of the bales during the preparation process by inserting a thermometer into the interior of the bale.

down to provide a suitable environment for the plants. Over the course of treatment, the internal temperature will drift slowly downward. Once you are below 80°F, the environment is suitable for the plants' roots.

Day 4: Repeat the Day 2 activity.

Day 5: Repeat the Day 1 activity.

Day 6: Repeat the Day 2 activity.

Days 7–9: Repeat the Day 1 activity, but use only ¼ cup of the lawn fertilizer.

Day 10: Check and record the internal temperature of the bale. Sprinkle 1 cup of the balanced (10-10-10) granular plant food across the top of the bale. Thoroughly water, as you have been doing daily.

Days 11–12: Check and record the internal temperature of the bale. Water thoroughly. If, on Day 12, the temperature has fallen below 80°F, the bales are ready to plant.

PREPARING BALES WITH ORGANIC FERTILIZERS

Day 1: Check and record the internal temperature of the bale; it will likely be around 80°F. Add 3 cups of the 12-0-0 granular blood meal, sprinkling it evenly over the top of the bale. Using a hose with no connector and a moderate water flow, add water evenly over the top of the bale for about one minute; you will see water emerging from the bottom of the bale. Note that the water will not visibly dissolve the granular material but will begin to push the material down into the structure of the bale.

Day 2: Check and record the internal temperature of the bale. Water the bale thoroughly from the top.

Day 3: Repeat the Day 1 activity. At this point, you should see the internal bale temperature begin to rise. The temperature should peak at approximately 120°F, which indicates the action of the nutrients on the bale components, breaking them down to provide a suitable environment for the plants. Over the course of treatment, the internal temperature will drift slowly downward, landing below 80°F, a safe temperature for the roots of your plants.

Day 4: Repeat the Day 2 activity.

Day 5: Repeat the Day 1 activity.

Day 6: Repeat the Day 2 activity.

Days 7–9: Repeat the Day 1 activity but use only ¾ cup of the blood meal.

Day 10: Check and record the internal temperature of the bale. Sprinkle 2 cups of the balanced (3-4-4) granular plant food across the top of the bale. Thoroughly water, as you have been doing daily.

Days 11–14: Check and record the internal temperature of the bale. Water thoroughly. If, on Day 14, the temperature has fallen below 80°F, the bales are ready to plant.

What Else Is Growing in My Bales?

Conditioned straw bales are constantly changing, and various things that you did not plant might emerge among the things that you did. Often, what you see in the morning is far different by midday, and gone completely by that evening.

Grasses. Though most of the seed tops are removed prior to baling, every bale I've planted sprouted grasses throughout the season. My experience is with germinating wheat, and I just leave it to add a little visual flair. If you wish, you can use scissors to cut the grass and use the clippings as mulch for bale tops.

High-Nitrogen Fertilizers

These are the fertilizers you can use for initial, standard bale treatment.

CONVENTIONAL OPTIONS:

- Lawn starter fertilizer: 29-0-4, $\frac{1}{2}$ cup per bale
- Ammonium nitrate: 34-0-0, $\frac{1}{2}$ cup per bale
- Calcium nitrate: 15-0-0, 1 cup per bale
- Ammonium sulfate: 21-0-0, $\frac{3}{4}$ cup per bale
- Urea: 46-0-0, $\frac{1}{4}$ cup per bale

ORGANIC OPTIONS:

- Blood meal: 12-0-0, 3 cups per bale
- Milorganite: 6-2-0, 3 cups per bale
- Fish emulsion: 5-1-1, 3 cups per bale
- Soybean meal: 7-2-1, 3 cups per bale
- Bat guano: 10-3-1, $1\frac{1}{2}$ cups per bale

Mushrooms. The real visual stars of the conditioned bales are the wild-looking mushrooms that pop out, often showing themselves the evening before, shooting spectacularly skyward overnight, then shriveling to nothingness in the sun the following day. The most common variety you'll find are called Inky Caps, and these mushrooms are not harmful to the plants. Since the "ink" can be used to write with and is quite black, they can make a mess — they stained my plant tags a bit.

Balanced Fertilizers

These fertilizers will sustain your plants throughout the growing season.

CONVENTIONAL OPTIONS:

- Granular fertilizer: 10-10-10, ½ cup per bale
- Water-soluble food: 20-20-20, ½ cup per bale

ORGANIC OPTIONS:

- Granular fertilizer: 3-4-4, 2 cups per bale
- Worm castings: 3-1-2, 2 cups per bale
- Alfalfa meal: 2-1-2, 2 cups per bale
- Composted manures: approximately 1-1-1, 3 cups per bale

PREPARING BALES WITHOUT FERTILIZER

THE SIMPLEST AND LEAST EXPENSIVE way to prepare your bales is simply to place them where you'll be gardening and water them daily. The watering alone will begin the internal breakdown process.

The main caveat for this method is that you'll likely need to allow for quite a bit more time — at least a full month — between the initial watering and the readiness of the bale for planting.

In my own trials, I found that the internal temperature of the bale didn't begin to rise significantly until Day 6. From that point until when I planted on Day 18, the temperature was about 10°F above ambient air temperature and remained steady. Contrast this with the 40°F temperature rise when using the pretreatment methods described above. The higher temperatures observed indicate faster structural breakdown of the interior of the bales. This explains the difference in preparation times: less than two weeks if you use fertilizer, a month or more when you use water alone.

Another caveat is that your plants may not thrive with this method. Whether it was because I didn't give the untreated bales enough time to break down, or because the fertilizer in the quick-start bales gave the seedlings a good initial boost, my trials showed that plants in the untreated bales did not grow as well as those planted in prepared bales.

CHAPTER FIVE

CARING FOR YOUR BALE GARDEN

Once the bales are planted with seedlings or seeds (see chapter 6 for how and what to grow in straw bales), regular care will keep things growing well and provide you with big, delicious harvests. It is important to provide appropriate support for tall growing or vining crops, and to water and feed the plants regularly.

Vertical support of the plants will help with air circulation and sun exposure, which in turn helps to minimize the onset and spread of fungal diseases. Regular watering is critical because of the large surface area of the bale, which leads to more evaporation and drainage. Regular feeding will compensate for the inherent lack of nutrients in the straw bales.

PROVIDING PLANT SUPPORT

STRAW BALE GARDENERS FACE some of the same decisions as container gardeners do, including when, if, and how to support their plants. For tall plants, such as indeterminate tomatoes (see page 75), some sort of vertical support is highly recommended to save space and improve yield. A single indeterminate tomato plant, grown unsupported, could end up covering an area many feet in diameter. Tomato plants whose foliage or fruit touches the ground are more susceptible to destructive soil-borne diseases and are more likely to be damaged by pests than those that are supported.

If you have chosen a permanent location for your bale garden, it may be worth investing time and materials in creating a trellis or support system that lasts many years. If, however, your garden will be located on a driveway, patio, or deck, temporary structures will suffice.

Temporary Supports

Most gardeners will likely want to try different crops each year, so the need for plant support will vary with each growing season. Gardeners who position their bales on decks, patios, or driveways will not be able to create the kind of permanent supports described on page 38. In each of these cases, temporary supports are in order.

STAKING

When bales are placed on soil: The simplest and least expensive kind of temporary support is an appropriately sized pole driven into the ground. Indeterminate tomatoes and pole beans can use as tall a pole as you can find and install; I use 8-foot plastic-coated poles with a metal core. For vegetables like eggplants, peppers, or shorter tomato varieties, go with 5- or 6-foot poles; these plants start out nearly 2 feet above the ground and grow 3 to 4 feet, and the pole should be driven about 1 foot into the ground.

You'll be planting each seedling in the center of the bale, and it will need to grow out to meet the installed support pole.

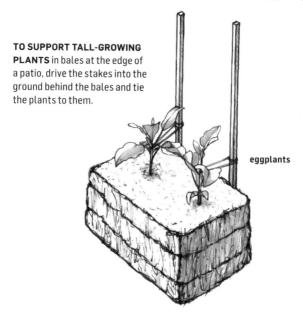

TO SUPPORT TALL-GROWING PLANTS in bales at the edge of a patio, drive the stakes into the ground behind the bales and tie the plants to them.

eggplants

Therefore, the plant must be supported early on, as it's trying to reach the pole; otherwise, its growth will be weak and vulnerable to breakage when the plant is older and heavier. This is especially true of tomatoes that are heavy with fruit. To create an early support, push a short stick or stake at an angle into the bale at the base of the plant, spanning the distance from the plant to the installed support pole. Use twine, strips of cloth, or your favorite equivalent to tie the plant to the short stake until it grows enough to meet the pole.

When bales are placed on hard surfaces: For many who decide to try bale gardening, one of the main attractions is the ability to site the garden in a sunny spot, even if it means growing on a deck, patio, or driveway. In situations where bales are placed on hard surfaces, though, staking requires a bit more creativity.

You can drive short stakes (4 to 5 feet long) into the bales themselves. This is effective for supporting peppers, eggplants, and shorter tomatoes. If you've placed the bales on a deck, lash the stakes to the deck railing. If you're gardening on a patio or driveway, place the bales at the edge of the paved surface and drive larger stakes (6 feet long) into the surrounding soil or lawn.

Another effective option is to position large, heavy containers of soil behind the bales and drive tall stakes into them. Be sure to bridge the gap between the base of the plant and the stake with a smaller stake, stick, or twine. Since the soil in the large pot can only provide so much support, you may need to prune the plant in the bale more frequently. Even with

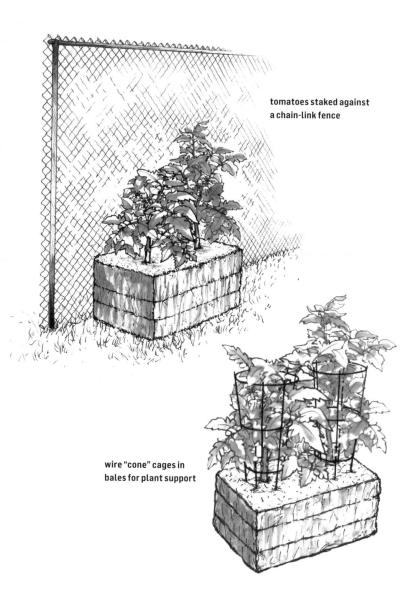

tomatoes staked against
a chain-link fence

wire "cone" cages in
bales for plant support

additional pruning, the plants and the bales themselves will likely tilt and lean as the season progresses, the bale breaks down, and the ripening vegetables grow heavy.

CAGES

The lightweight, 3- to 4-foot-tall wire cones sold as tomato cages are useful for keeping shorter, vertically grown plants controlled in straw bales. Their use should be limited to dwarf or determinate tomatoes; peppers; eggplant; the various compact bush-type, short-vine cucumbers and squash; and ground cherries — all of which top out at 3 to 4 feet tall. Cages can topple under the weight of mature plants and the lack of foundation when the bale breaks down. Staking the cage will help keep it (and the plant) upright later in the season. It's best to drive the stake into the ground behind the bale, if possible; otherwise, drive it into the bale itself or into a heavy pot of dirt placed behind the bale.

TRELLIS VARIATIONS

Some crops, such as long-vined beans, tall-growing peas, and most cucumbers, will benefit from a trellis behind the bales. There are a variety of trellis products on the market, but trellises are also quite simple to make yourself. Again, a significant limiting factor is whether or not the supporting poles can be driven into soil to anchor the trellis. If this isn't possible for your setup, lash tall poles to the deck railing or other nearby structure. For a freestanding trellis, place large containers of soil on either side of the bale and sink poles into them.

Be aware of the growth limits of the particular plants you wish to support. Since you are already starting the plants at an increased height, be sure to add this to the anticipated height of the plants and ensure that the trellis can accommodate the difference.

Permanent Supports

Because of the potential cost and physical labor involved, you may want to try out straw bale gardening on a smaller, more temporary scale to see how it works for you before you embark

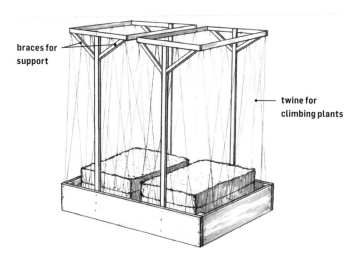

braces for support

twine for climbing plants

ONE EXAMPLE OF A TRELLIS, suitable for long-term or permanent use, is shown here. The raised walls add protection for the bales, and the vertical structure and twine provide support for climbing plants. There are endless possibilities for design and creativity based on the needs of the vegetables.

on creating permanent supports. However, once you are ready to commit to the up-front costs and labor, permanent supports for your vertical crops can be very effective and need only be installed once.

One such system consists of parallel rows of fencing anchored at the ends by tall, solid poles, such as steel T-bar poles. The end poles need to be driven deeply into the ground to effectively support crops with heavy fruit set. Once your end poles are in place, connect them with 2×4s attached at the top of the poles; these will help keep the end poles vertical, especially when the system is supporting heavy crops. At this point, you have three options:

- Use heavy-gauge electric fence wire to connect the end spans, at vertical intervals of 1 foot.
- Drop lengths of strong twine or heavy-gauge wire from the top board toward the bale tops wherever you will have a tall-growing plant. If using lighter twine, anchor it at the base of the plant by tying it to a short stake driven into the bale; this will keep it from blowing away from the plant in the wind when your garden is just getting started.
- Run a length of concrete-reinforcing wire or livestock panel down the rows just behind the bales, well secured onto the end poles.

For each of these support methods, the plants are easily wound around or through the wiring or caging, and the secure anchor posts and robust materials ensure tidy vertical growth. The continuous span across the entire row also allows for some creative options for vine training, such as espalier.

WAYS TO WATER AND FERTILIZE

As noted in chapter 1, straw bales are essentially large sponges that soak up water and nutrients and allow the root systems of plants to infiltrate and absorb what they need. Because straw bales are so porous, however, and because they're most often placed in direct sun, they must be watered frequently. Frequent watering creates the need for regular feeding, though, as the plants' roots can absorb only so much at a given time and excess nutrients are washed out of the bales along with the water.

Straw bales can absorb several gallons of water, so be sure to choose a watering method that isn't too labor-intensive. It's fine to use a watering can if you have only a few bales; for larger gardens, plan ahead and place your bales within reach of a hose. For initial bale preparation and for watering mature plants, a moderate flow from a hose without an attachment works fine.

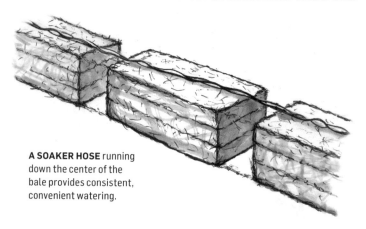

A SOAKER HOSE running down the center of the bale provides consistent, convenient watering.

For bales that have been recently prepped and seeded, use a spray nozzle with a gentle setting, to avoid displacing the planting medium and seeds. Direct the water at the base of the plants, keeping foliage dry; wet foliage in cool, cloudy weather can bring on fungal diseases and rot.

Drip irrigation or soaker hoses are also an option, especially for rows of bales. Hook up drip lines or soaker hoses to automatic timers, to calibrate water delivery and ensure sufficient moisture for each bale. Position the soaker hose or the transmitters to sit on top of the bales. For bales that are direct-seeded (see page 46), it may be best to lay the soaker hose in between the bales prior to adding the top layer of planting medium.

WATERING AND FERTILIZING SCHEDULE

THE WATERING FREQUENCY for straw bale gardens depends on the amount of sun they receive, the maturity of the plants, the temperature, and the weather. Remember that the porous structure of bales means that overwatering is virtually impossible: providing some water daily can't hurt. To fine-tune your watering, though, you can simply stick your finger into the bale to see how quickly it is drying out. The plants will tell you if they're dry by wilting, especially in the midafternoon heat. Adequate water is especially critical for newly planted seedlings and recently germinated seeds. Pay particular attention to watering once fruit sets on the plants; insufficient watering during fruit-set can lead to problems such as blossom-end rot on tomatoes.

All of that watering causes plant nutrients to move through the bales quickly. Applying small amounts of balanced fertilizer on a weekly basis is a good strategy, at least as a starting point. As the weather becomes warmer and watering becomes more frequent, additional fertilizing could be necessary. Learn to "read" your plants to assess whether they're receiving the nutrients they need. Rich, green foliage and good flower and fruit production are signs of happy plants. Faded or yellowing foliage can be a sign of a plant that's lacking nutrients. Loads of foliage but few flowers can mean the plant is receiving lots of nitrogen but perhaps not enough phosphorus, potassium, and/ or micronutrients. See chapter 7 for more information about troubleshooting your garden.

....

Fertilizer from Urine?

You may have heard or read about using urine as fertilizer and wondered, can you really pee on your bales? Of course you can, strictly speaking! But how beneficial is it? Human urine actually has an N-P-K ratio of about 11-1-2.5, or very similar to the starter fertilizers that are used for bale conditioning. The high nitrogen content means that it is best to consider urine to augment the conditioning stage, and stop direct use after the bale is planted. After that, you are on your own — urine can be composted, and the compost used as post-planting fertilizing. There is a wealth of resources online to do your own research into the matter, if you're so inclined.

....

CHAPTER SIX

WHAT TO GROW AND HOW TO GROW IT

Most of the hard work is now done. You've purchased the bales, put them into place, and prepared them. You've decided whether to support the plants and, if so, installed the structures. Now for the fun parts: planting, growing, and harvesting!

Pretty much any vegetable can be grown in straw bales. In fact, the technique may be just the answer for attempting vegetables that haven't succeeded in your gardening past. For example, carrots and leeks, which can be challenging to grow in poor or inappropriate garden soil, are perfect candidates for growing in bales. Consider bales as an ideal growing medium, perhaps the best you've ever had to work with, and let your garden include those beloved edibles that you've previously avoided.

TRANSPLANT OR DIRECT-SEED?

THE DECISION OF WHETHER TO TRANSPLANT prestarted seedlings or to sow seeds directly is the same in straw bale gardening as it is in other forms of gardening. You'll need to consider how long a crop takes to mature in your climate and whether the crop tolerates being transplanted. As with in-ground gardening, it's also important to time your planting with your last-frost date in mind, to avoid setting out plants too early; the website for the National Weather Service (weather.gov) has reliable data for this. And, of course, when you're growing in straw bales you'll need to coordinate your bale preparation timeline with your plans for planting.

Crops best suited for transplant are those with extremely tiny seeds, very slow initial growth or extended germination times, or a need for elevated temperature. Some of these can certainly be direct-seeded, but harvest would be significantly delayed and yields reduced. In contrast, it is a waste of effort and valuable indoor space to start crops indoors that are easy and successful to grow from direct seeding.

Crops best suited for direct seeding tend to possess one or more of the following characteristics: large seeds, rapid germination and growth, and sensitivity to being transplanted.

Transplanting Seedlings

If possible, plant seedlings on a cloudy day to minimize transplant stress. If you must plant when it's sunny, work later in the day to avoid setting out seedlings in the hot sun.

Using a trowel or another cultivating tool, create a hollow in the bale that is sufficient to contain the root ball, tuber, clove, or slip. (See the crop-specific planting and spacing information on pages 47–74.) Even when the bales are ready to plant, the straw will likely still be quite stiff; it will take some effort with your tool to create the depression, and you may need to plunge the tool into the bale and pull out some of the straw. Insert the plant into the hole and fill in around it with a compost-rich planting medium (see pages 13–14), leveling it with the top of the bale, and water it well. If you removed some of the straw when creating the hollow, you can use it as mulch around the newly planted seedling.

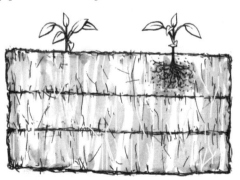

cutaway view
of a partially
planted bale

Direct Seeding

After the bale is prepared, apply a level, 2-inch layer of the planting medium (see pages 13–14) to the top of the bale and firm it down gently. Carefully water the medium and the top of the bale so that both are well moistened. Create holes or rows, as recommended for each crop type, using the spacing indicated for each crop (see pages 47–74). Following planting, ensure that the seeds are covered with planting medium at the appropriate depth indicated for that crop; then firm the planting mix gently and water lightly.

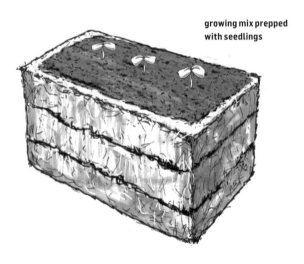

growing mix prepped
with seedlings

STRAW BALE GARDENING

 = direct seed   = transplant

THE HEIGHT OF STRAW BALES makes planting seeds easy, fun, and far less of a hardship on the back. Follow the guidelines on the seed packets, and my recommendations here, for seed spacing and depth. Uneven or unexpected weather could mean the need to go back and fill in any areas where germination was lower than hoped.

Beans

Beans are wonderful for providing high yields in relation to the growing area. The easiest to grow are bush beans, which grow 1 foot or so tall. The short, compact growth habit means that there is no need to consider plant support. The plants near the edge of the bale will eventually flop over a bit with the weight of the beans, but that won't be a problem if you pick them regularly. An added and significant advantage is the elevation of the plants when it is time to pick. Gardeners will agree that bending over and picking long rows of beans is quite unpleasant. The extra elevation provided by the bale will mean delicious servings of beans without the back pain.

Some gardeners think that pole bean varieties and runner (or half-runner) beans are even tastier than bush beans. If you choose to grow pole or runner beans in bales, it is best to position them toward the back of the garden so that they don't shade other plants. It is also important to provide a tall trellis or poles for the vines to climb.

SOWING: For bush beans, plant the seeds 1 inch deep and 4 to 6 inches apart each way, starting 4 to 6 inches from the edge of the bale. Each bale planted this way will hold approximately 15 bean seeds. The slightly elevated internal heat of the bale will aid in quick germination, and the excellent drainage of the top soilless planting medium layer should eliminate seed rotting, as long as the soil temperature is above 70°F. With the spacing recommended here, there will be no need to thin seedlings. If there are some "blanks" (and there will be, since no seeds have a 100 percent germination rate), just fill in with an additional seed.

If you wish to try pole or runner beans, plant them down the center of the bale in a single row and provide poles or a trellis system at the back of the bale. Once the seeds germinate, insert a short plant stake at the back of the plant at an angle toward the pole or trellis so that the plant will find the tall supports once they start to vine.

Beets

Beets are very easy and rewarding crops that grow well in cool weather. I actually like the beet greens just as much as the beets themselves. Time the bale preparation so that you can direct-seed the beets in early spring. A minimum temperature of 40°F is required for germination. In most cases, beet "seeds" are actually seed balls containing multiple seeds, resulting in multiple plants. The exceptions are those varieties that are labeled "monogerm," which will produce one plant per seed.

SOWING: Beet seeds can be planted as close as 3 inches apart, and in rows 4 inches apart, at a depth of ¾ inch. You will be

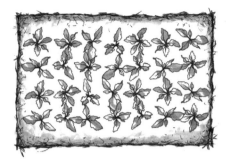

appropriately spaced
beet seedlings

able to fit 40 or more seeds per bale. When the beet seedlings are a few inches tall, you will note that there are multiple seedlings where most seeds were planted (especially if you have seeded the bales intensively). Cut the extra plants carefully at the soil level, taking the thinned plants to eat as greens. Manage the spacing to aim for the beet size you seek: the wider the spacing, the larger the beet at maturity.

Beet Seedlings

A different approach to beets that results in nicely sized, uniform roots is to start them indoors very early. They can be seeded thickly into small containers; then, upon thinning, the seedlings can be transplanted into individual cells in flats. (I like to use stiff plastic "plug flats" that contain 50 cells in a roughly 1 by 2 foot area, but there are countless options available.) After a few weeks, when they are growing vigorously, each plant can be popped out of the plug, positioned into small depressions in the bale, and firmed into each hole using planting mix. By spacing the beet plugs with 3 inches in all directions, you can maximize the surface area of the bale: each bale will provide up to 50 perfect, sweet beets.

Cabbage Family

 BROCCOLI, BRUSSELS SPROUTS, CABBAGE, CAULIFLOWER

It's best to start broccoli, Brussels sprouts, cabbage, and cauliflower in straw bales by transplanting seedlings. These plants prefer relatively cool weather and are best planted early for ripening before the intense heat of midsummer. Late-summer planting for a fall crop is also possible.

Brussels sprout seedlings

 COLLARD GREENS, KALE

Collard greens and kale can be direct-seeded for harvest of small, tender greens for salads and stir-fries. Collards and kale improve in flavor, becoming much sweeter, following a frost. These are also the largest-growing greens, so the more widely spaced they are, the more vigorous and productive each individual plant will become.

DENSITY: Both the eventual size and the yield of plants in the cabbage family will be affected by the plant density per bale. For a starting point, consider planting two Brussels sprouts seedlings; two cabbage seedlings; or four broccoli, cauliflower, collard, or kale seedlings, evenly spaced, in one bale. Closer spacing will mean smaller heads or less harvestable leaves. Direct seeding of collards and kale can be made in bands or sprinkled throughout. As the plants mature, use the thinnings in salads or cooked dishes.

PLANTING: Use the technique for transplanting seedlings in bales described on page 45.

Carrots

Carrots, so challenging for gardeners with heavy or rocky clay soil, are far more successful when grown in straw bales. As the center of the bale breaks down over time, a perfect destination develops for the growing carrots. The result will be a bale stocked with straight, uniform, delicious carrots that are easy to harvest.

SOWING: Cover the prepped bale with a layer of planting medium a few inches deep; then firm and gently water. Drag a finger through the top to create rows 1 inch deep, a few inches apart, and sow seeds thinly across each row. Try to leave a few inches between seeds. Sprinkle planting medium over the seeded rows, firm it, and gently water.

You will soon notice germination of the seeds in the rows, though it will likely be irregular. If the surface dried out in spots, there will be delays in growth or early death of tiny, dry seedlings. Lightly draping floating row cover (frost cloth) over the bale during germination helps maintain more even soil moisture. Once germination is complete, thin the seedlings to allow for 2 inches between plants. Continue to be vigilant about adequate soil moisture; the roots are very shallow early on, so watch for drying, especially on hot afternoons.

Corn

Corn can certainly be grown in straw bales, but the ultimate size and nutrient needs of the plants create challenges that a gardener may wish to avoid. Because most varieties of corn grow very tall and need sufficient spacing to provide adequate water and nutrition for each plant, it's best to try corn in bales on a very small scale at first to see how you do with it. One other idea is to try some of the very short corn varieties, such as certain popcorn varieties.

Remember that the plants will already be quite far off the ground when seeded, meaning a 6-foot corn plant will be 8 feet tall or more. The open structure of the bale also provides less of an anchor for the plant when compared to heavier garden soil, so lodging (bending or tipping) is even more likely. You'll need to stake or trellis corn plants and regularly tie them to keep them vertical.

SOWING: Plant single corn seeds 1 inch deep, leaving 6 inches or more between seeds; the maximum for one bale is two rows of 6 plants, staggered, for a total of 12 plants. If each plant provides a maximum of two ears, optimum conditions will give you two dozen ears of corn.

Cucumbers and Melons

Most varieties of cucumbers and melons are vining types that will take up a large area around the bales. It won't take the germinated seedlings very long to cascade down the bale in all directions, taking up significant space and clogging walking lanes. A good alternative is to set up a rear trellis and wind the vines up the support.

There are two reasons to start cucumbers and melons from seed directly planted into the bales: first, the seeds germinate quickly; second, the plants grow rapidly. The seedlings of these crops also resent disturbance and take time to settle into their new surroundings. However, if you live in a cold climate with a short growing season, you can start cucumber or melon seeds indoors in individual pots and then carefully transplant the seedlings into the bales.

Compared with cucumbers, melons typically yield less. However, because the mature fruits of some melon varieties are quite heavy, they may slip off the vines when they're fully

cucumber seedlings

ripe. One way to keep the melons on the vines until ripe is to affix slings to the trellis to support the developing fruit.

SOWING: Plant seeds 1 inch deep, three seeds per bale, equally spaced.

Eggplant

If you love eggplant but have been disappointed with your results in the past, you'll be pleasantly surprised by how well this vegetable grows in straw bales. Eggplants, like peppers, grow more vigorously and have greater yields when their roots are warm. The plants have a spread of 1 to 2 feet and a mature height of 3 to 4 feet.

Freshly grown eggplants are not at all bitter, and the flavor is quite consistent variety to variety. In deciding which types to grow, think about color and fruit shape. Eggplants come in a variety of skin colors: white, green, pink, lavender, and nearly black, with swirled or striped options as well. Shape variations run from nearly flattened to perfectly round, and from the

eggplant seedlings

familiar teardrop shapes to the slender, skinny varieties commonly used in Asian cuisine.

DENSITY: Because of the vigor and spread of the plants, limit each bale to two plants.

PLANTING: Eggplant seedlings, purchased or homegrown by starting indoors, are planted into bales exactly as described for tomatoes (page 74). They are frost-sensitive and so should not be planted until nighttime temperatures are above 32°F.

Garlic, Shallots, and Potato Onions

Garlic comes in two main types: hardneck (larger cloves, easier to peel, shorter shelf life) and softneck (smaller cloves, longer shelf life). Like garlic, shallots and potato onions (both of which are sometimes called multiplier onions) grow in clusters. It is important to read the source bulb catalog to determine suitability for your climate and optimum planting time.

Onion-family bulbs do well in straw bales and, in most areas of the United States, are planted in the fall. If you have already planted your bales with other crops earlier in the season, you can purchase new bales and prepare them so that they are ready when you purchase or receive the bulbs. Though it is possible to plant onion-family bulbs in used bales as a succession crop, the structure of the bales is typically quite broken down by the end of the growing season. One solution to this would be to place the bales in homemade wooden frames, which keep the material together.

If they have not been treated with a sprout inhibitor, store-bought garlic bulbs can be separated into individual cloves and then planted; look for "organic" or "untreated" on the label to find such bulbs. However, even if you find an organic variety of garlic in the grocery store, it may not be suitable for your particular climate. Refer to seed catalogs, and purchase garlic bulbs either by mail order or at your local garden center.

DENSITY: Space garlic cloves, shallot bulbs, or potato onion bulbs 5 to 6 inches apart throughout the bale. Yield potential is very high per bale.

PLANTING: Create 2-inch-deep depressions throughout the top of the bale; this will be very easy if you are reusing bales that contained other plants in the spring. Press the individual cloves or bulbs into the depressions, ensuring that the pointy (growing) end is up and the flatter (root) end down. Cover with some planting medium until the medium is level with the bale surface; firm the bale top, and water gently.

Herbs

Herbs tend to be less fussy than many vegetables. They are also less dependent on high levels of fertilizer; in fact, some gardeners believe that the intensity of essential oils in herbs is enhanced by leaner growing conditions and less water. Because of their strong aromas and flavors, they're also less likely to be attacked by pests than vegetables are.

You can either dedicate full bales to single types of herbs, mix and match the types to create one-bale herb gardens, or spot herbs here and there among your vegetables. Herbs tend to be used sparingly in the kitchen, so one plant of a particular herb type may suffice. Basil may be an exception, especially if you like to make large quantities of pesto.

assorted herb seedlings

Herbs with small seeds (basil, oregano, parsley, rosemary, sage, and thyme) are best grown from transplanted seedlings. Basil, oregano, sage, and thyme are quick and easy when started indoors. Simply sowing in moistened soilless mix, barely covering and providing a warm place works just fine. Parsley can be quite slow, and rosemary has very low germination. Herb plants are plentiful at garden centers in the spring for those who don't wish to sow seeds indoors.

Herbs that are best for direct seeding are those with large seeds, rapid growth, and/or a dislike of being transplanted; these include borage, chervil, chives, cilantro, and dill. Many also tend to be quite short-lived, particularly when it becomes warmer. A packet of seeds allows you to grow several crops on a particular bale — just toss the plants when they are looking tired, and reseed.

DENSITY: Consider the mature size of the various herb types when figuring on spacing. Most healthy herb plants will spread to at least 1 foot in diameter. Position the taller herbs at the back of the bale.

PLANTING: For seedlings, use the transplanting techniques described on page 45. For seeds, herb seed packets usually provide all of the information needed for depth of seeding and recommended spacing. If you have an overabundance of seedlings after germination, gently pluck them out of the bale top and pot them up; share the pots with friends and family, or place them in other areas of your garden.

BASIL, OREGANO, PARSLEY, ROSEMARY, SAGE, THYME

Herbs with small seeds (basil, oregano, parsley, rosemary, sage, and thyme) are best grown from transplanted seedlings. Basil, oregano, sage, and thyme are quick and easy when started indoors. Simply sowing in moistened soilless mix, barely covering and providing a warm place works just fine. Parsley can be quite slow, and rosemary has very low germination. Herb plants are plentiful at garden centers in the spring for those who don't wish to sow seeds indoors.

PLANTING: Use the technique for transplanting seedlings in bales described on page 45.

BORAGE, CHERVIL, CHIVES, CILANTRO, DILL

Herbs that are best for direct seeding are those with large seeds, rapid growth, and/or a dislike of being transplanted; these include borage, chervil, chives, cilantro, and dill. Many also tend to be quite short-lived, particularly when it becomes warmer. A packet of seeds allows you to grow several crops on a particular bale — just toss the plants when they are looking tired, and reseed.

PLANTING: Herb seed packets usually provide all of the information needed for depth of seeding and recommended spacing. After germination, the herb seedlings will probably need to be thinned to avoid overcrowding. Feel free to gently transplant extra seedlings into pots or other containers, or they can be discarded.

Leeks

Leeks, a true culinary treasure, tend to be expensive. They can also be hard to find, and even if you do find them in stores, they may have been grown in clay or sand and therefore have lots of grit embedded in the edible white shaft. All of these factors make leeks an attractive candidate for your straw bale garden.

DENSITY: Space leek seedlings 4 to 6 inches apart in rows 6 inches apart. This will translate to 30 to 40 leeks per bale.

PLANTING: Leeks are best started from seed indoors and transplanted into bales as seedlings. To produce the edible white stem, leeks need to be blanched (that is, hidden from the sun); you can do this by hilling soil around the growing plants.

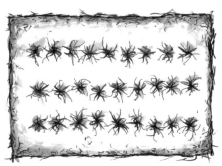

leek seedlings

Any part of the leek plant that grows beneath the surface of the soil will be white; the deeper the seedling is planted, the more white leek shaft will result. Create rows in the bales that are 6 inches apart and 8 inches deep using a cultivator or trowel. Add 2 inches of planting medium at the bottom of the rows, and gently water the medium. Poke 1-inch holes in the medium and insert the leek seedlings, allowing 6 inches between plants. Gently firm the medium around the plant, ensuring that some green emerges from the top of the soil, and water the seedlings gently.

As the leeks grow, add planting medium to the rows on a weekly basis so that just the top inch of the leek plant remains above the soil line. Eventually, you will find that the medium in the rows is level with the top of the bale — at this point, just keep the leeks well watered and fertilized.

 ## Okra

Okra is a member of the hibiscus family, as is demonstrated by the characteristically flat, round, sunny flowers produced before the pods set. It is very easy to grow, from direct seeding (in climates with at least three months of warm temperatures) or indoor-started seedlings (in climates with a short growing season). Direct-sown okra germinates best when the temperature is around 65°F and grows best when the nighttime temperature is around 65°F and daytime temperature is around 85°F. If you must start the seedlings ahead of time indoors, handle them gently when you transplant them to avoid disturbing the taproot.

okra seedlings

SOWING: For direct seeding, plant the seeds 1 inch deep and 12 inches apart. Limit your seeding to a maximum of four plants per bale. Okra is a tall plant that will become heavy once the fruit sets, so it is important to provide support for the plants using one of the staking or trellising ideas provided in chapter 5.

  ## Onions

Onions are planted from sets (small bulbs), or indoor-started or purchased seedlings. There is great diversity in onions for mature size, sweetness/hotness, bulb color, and a parameter called daylight sensitivity, so be sure to select varieties suitable for your climate. If you're starting onions from sets, make sure the variety is suitable for your garden.

DENSITY: Whether you're starting with sets or seedlings, space onions 2 to 6 inches apart, depending on the size of the particular variety. If you dedicate a single bale to onions, this means a harvest of up to 60 small onions.

PLANTING: Create depressions in the bale 6 inches apart and deep enough for the tip of the set to be level with the bale surface. For seedlings, create furrows a few inches deep, fill with the planting medium, lay the transplants on the surface, and gently push them into the furrow, roots down, spaced 6 inches apart. After planting the sets or seedlings, add planting medium if necessary so that the surface of the bale is level. Water the bale gently.

Peas

Most gardeners crave fresh peas, which certainly can grow well in straw bales. The main decisions are whether to go with bush-type peas, which grow a few feet tall and need less support, or taller-growing vining types like the original Sugar Snap, which require a trellis system. Peas also come and go quite quickly and never seem to produce as much as you wish for. To satisfy true pea lovers, it may be useful to set up a solid line of several bales for the pea crop.

A great way to provide sufficient support for shorter-growing (bush-type) pea varieties is to stick thin, 2-foot-tall tree or bush branches into the bale at random 6- to 12-inch intervals. As the peas germinate and grow, they will climb up the branches and along the twigs, preventing a tangled mass of plants and making the pods easier to find and harvest.

SOWING: Plant peas 1½ inches deep into prepared bales. Short-growing peas can be randomly scattered, then thinned, allowing a few inches between plants. Insert the support branches after planting.

Plant tall, vining-type peas 1½ inches deep in a double row, with the seeds 2 to 3 inches apart. Separate the rows by about 6 inches. Then insert sticks or twigs along the row at an acute angle, leading from the bale to the rear trellis system. This will provide a means for the growing pea plants to reach the trellis so that they can then complete their tall climb upward.

Peppers

Because of the increased soil temperature, peppers are often much more productive when grown in containers than when they're planted in the garden. Given the similar conditions, it stands to reason that peppers grown in straw bales would do equally well; my trials for growing peppers in straw bales were very successful, producing heavy yields of colorful, sweet bells on vigorous, healthy plants.

SWEET PEPPERS

Sweet peppers (which contain little to no capsaicin, hence little to no heat) come in a rainbow of colors and vary in shape from flat and tomato-like to the familiar bells to the elongated, sweet banana type and Italian frying peppers. With an endless array of options in both hybrid and open pollinated categories, and with costs of ripe sweet peppers always high, growing them is a superb use of garden space and well worth the minimal effort. Decide which shape, size, and color best fit your needs, since the flavor of peppers is quite uniform between varieties.

Most sweet peppers share a very vigorous growth habit, forming a bush about 2 feet wide and up to 4 feet tall by the end of the season. Unlike tomato plants, pepper plants have brittle branches: many a pepper will be lost when unsupported branches snap under their weight. Using cone-shaped cages (see page 37) is a perfect way to avoid this issue.

DENSITY: Because of the vigor and spread of the plants, limit your planting to two pepper plants per bale.

PLANTING: Plant pepper seedlings, purchased or homegrown by starting indoors, into bales exactly as described for tomatoes (see page 74). Like tomatoes, peppers are frost-sensitive and so should not be planted until nighttime temperatures are above 32°F.

HOT PEPPERS

sweet pepper seedlings

The possibilities for hot peppers significantly exceed those for sweet peppers. Not only are there many examples in each hot pepper category (*Capsicum annuum*, *C. baccatum*, *C. frutescens*, and *C. chinense* are the most commonly grown), but fruit size, shape and color, plant habit, and especially heat levels all vary widely among the varieties. Hot peppers share with sweet peppers a love of well-warmed root zones. Most hot pepper varieties are virtual pepper machines, so you may not need many plants unless you are a true hot pepper addict.

DENSITY: Knowing your variety is important for determining planting density per bale. Most commonly grown types, such as jalapeño, serrano, and habanero, are very vigorous and should be limited to two plants per bale. The small, colorful ornamental types can be planted much closer, perhaps staggered at six plants per bale.

PLANTING: Plant hot pepper seedlings into bales exactly as described for tomatoes (see page 74). Like tomatoes, they are frost-sensitive and so should not be planted until nighttime temperatures are above 32°F. If you choose to plant more densely, try to avoid planting close to the bale edges and be sure to create the planting holes at equal distances in the bale.

Potatoes

Growing potatoes in straw bales takes a fun garden crop and makes it even better. The digging-for-gold aspect of potatoes is enhanced by putting the bounty all in one spot. Once the plants die back, the spuds are somewhere in the now-crumbling oblong; to strike pay dirt, all you need is just some careful digging around.

Though you can use store-bought potatoes that are sprouting, there is such a diversity of colors and flavors that it is well worth purchasing your seed potatoes from a commercial source. Commercially sold seed potatoes are also more certain to be free of diseases. Grow your crop in newly conditioned bales, or reuse bales that were planted with spring crops and are well broken down in the middle.

DENSITY: Potatoes are heavy feeders, and the vines spread widely. If you crowd them, the yield will be disappointing. Plan on three to four plants per bale at most. Well-grown bales of potatoes will yield 20 pounds or more at the end of the season.

PLANTING: Plant whole small potatoes or sections of larger specimens; each section should contain at least one eye. Create 6- to 12-inch depressions in the bale. Place a seed potato into each depression. Cover the seed potatoes with sufficient mix so that they are beneath 2 inches of material. As the plants sprout, gradually add more mix until the tops of the bales are level.

Over time, the plants will emerge from the bale, becoming quite large. There is no need to support the vigorous, flopping plants. Once the plants begin to die back, typically 2 to 3 months after planting, carefully explore the bales to find the potatoes.

Radishes

Radishes are one of the easiest and earliest crops to grow; committing a straw bale for an early radish crop is a great idea for spring salads, and you can leave the bale for longer-season crops once the harvest is complete. Whether you dedicate a full or partial bale to radishes, it is easier to scatter the seeds than to plant them singly.

SOWING: Broadcast the seed thinly over the planting medium of a prepared bale; then sprinkle additional mix onto the top, covering the seeds to a depth of ½ inch. Firm the bale top, and gently apply water. A week or so after germination, use scissors to thin any places that are planted too thickly. For good-sized radish production, allow a few inches between plants.

Scallions

Scallions, also known as green onions or occasionally spring onions, find many uses in the kitchen and are easily grown from seed. Parts of straw bales can be dedicated to their growth, and they can also be planted successively until it gets too hot.

SOWING: Plant scallion seeds ½-inch deep in rows, or scatter them. Once they germinate, thin to allow 1 to 2 inches between the plants.

Spring Greens

Spring greens (which include arugula, Asian greens, lettuce, and spinach) are easy and quick to grow. They do best in cool weather and can be spaced quite closely. One or two bales will supply plenty of salads for weeks. You may wish to have something in mind for the bales afterward, however, because once the weather heats up, the greens bolt and become bitter. Although you can purchase spring greens as seedlings or start them indoors to provide transplants, it is just as easy to directly seed them onto prepared bales.

SOWING: Plant the seeds shallowly and randomly across the top of the prepared bale or in shallow rows. Keep them in clusters or rows by variety, or mix them as you wish. If you find that you planted them too densely, thin them by cutting the extras and use the leaves in salads.

Strawberries

This most wonderful early summer crop is worth a try for straw bales. A great advantage of growing them in bales is apparent at picking time, when the elevation provided by the bales brings the treasure much closer to the picker. The height also puts some distance between the berries and potential thieves such as slugs and rabbits.

There are many varieties to choose from, but almost all will fall into one of two types: June-bearing and ever-bearing (also known as day-neutral). As the name indicates, June-bearing varieties produce one large crop early in the growing season and send out numerous runners. Ever-bearing varieties continually bear fruit from early summer to autumn (though production does taper off with time); they produce fewer runners. Strawberries are best treated as an annual, so I suggest trying particularly suitable varieties on a small scale to see how they do in your particular climate.

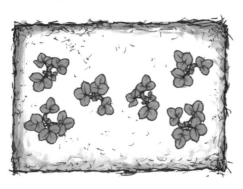

strawberry seedlings

DENSITY: Plan on spacing the plants 1 foot apart; the need for space will limit you to about six plants per bale.

PLANTING: You can obtain strawberry plants from local garden centers or by mail order. Dig 6-inch depressions into the prepared bales, settle the plants into the holes, and add the planting medium, covering the roots and filling in the holes until level after firming. Water them well and regularly. The plants will produce runners that will cascade over the bale sides.

 ## Summer and Winter Squash

Summer squash (including yellow squash and zucchini) are tender skinned, quick growing, and notably prolific. It's easy to grow them from direct seeding in straw bales. Although most summer squash varieties are bush types, they actually do expand and spread a few feet from the plant base over the growing season. They may start centered on the straw bales, but it won't take long for them to extend beyond and over the edges. Unplanted bales surrounding the crop can provide "tables" onto which the squash plants can run, keeping the squash easily visible and pickable.

Winter squash (including acorn squash, pumpkins, and spaghetti squash among many other types) are hard shelled and slow growing. But they are also easy to grow from direct seeding. For the most part, they are very long vined, and that is the chief consideration when growing them in straw bales. Since the vines travel great distances, consider using landscape fabric on the ground between the bales so that they have a place to run. Separating the winter squash bales into a less populated garden area could also be helpful. Small-fruited squash can be grown up a trellis.

SOWING: For all types of squash, plant two squash seeds per planting hole (slightly separated) 1 inch deep into prepared bales. Visually divide the bale in half, and center the planting in each half. Water well and watch for germination. If both plants germinate in each planting site, snip away the smaller one. Replant any germination failures. Following germination and the extra plant snip, aim for two squash plants per bale.

....

Succession Planting

The term *succession planting* refers to following one crop with another in the same growing season. Straw bales used for quick-growing crops such as spring greens, peas, and even bush beans should still be in pretty good shape for succession planting once the spent plants are removed. Consider reusing the bales for rapid-growing direct-seeded crops like beans, squash, or cucumbers. If you live in an area with a long growing season, you can plant potatoes in used bales.

Even mature bales that hold long-growing plants like eggplant, peppers, and tomatoes are fine for fall greens or onion-family relatives that are fall-planted, such as garlic, if they are confined in a wooden frame. The frames will prevent the bales from totally collapsing and keep them in bounds throughout the winter, into spring.

....

 Sweet Potatoes

Although they are an entirely different species, sweet potatoes are similar to white potatoes in that the edible tubers develop from the plant's roots inside of the bale. The main growing differences are their temperature preferences (sweet potatoes like it hot, while regular potatoes prefer cool temperatures), and how they're planted. Unlike potatoes (which are started from small seed potatoes or pieces with eyes), sweet potatoes are started from seedlings, or slips, that are embedded into the bale. You can purchase sweet potato slips at some local garden centers or via mail order. You can also start them yourself from sweet potatoes; this of course takes extra time, so be sure to plan for it if you go this route.

DENSITY: Plan on using four sweet potato slips per straw bale, with equal spacing between them. Each slip can produce 2 pounds or more of sweet potatoes, so your total yield of a planted bale may be as much as 10 pounds.

PLANTING: Create depressions in the prepared straw bale so that the roots of the slips sit at least 4 inches below the surface. Set the slips in by the roots and add planting medium to the hole, completely covering the roots. Firm the slip so that the surface of the bale is level. Gently water around each plant until well saturated; it is important that the young plants stay well watered. Soon the roots will stretch and the vines will grow long enough to spread over and around the bale.

 **Swiss Chard**

Like collard greens and kale (see page 50), Swiss chard is fine for salads but even better in stir fries and smoothies. Chard prefers cools weather and is typically grown as a spring crop, but it often lasts throughout the summer, well into fall.

SOWING: Plant seeds shallowly, 6 to 8 inches apart, and thin to the desired spacing once they germinate. Harvest the outer leaves throughout the season, and the center of the plant replenishes the greens continuously.

 Tomatillos and Ground Cherries

Quite weedy in growth habit, tomatillos and ground cherries share a love of heat with their cousin, the tomato (see facing page). However, they tend to be more spreading plants that are tricky to keep under control.

Ground cherries yield very heavily even when just a single plant is grown. Tomatillos, though, need to be pollinated with other tomatillo plants (a single plant will flower but not produce fruit); numerous types of bees, and even hummingbirds, will carry out the task.

One straw bale with two tomatillo plants will work just fine. Tomatillos can grow quite tall, so a combination of stake and cage will keep the plants under control. A cage should suffice with ground cherries, which typically top out at 3 feet.

DENSITY: Because of their vigor and spread, tomatillos should be limited to two plants per bale. If you really love them, you can grow three ground cherry plants in a single bale, but be ready to deal with the bountiful harvest. Seedlings of either are planted just like tomatoes.

PLANTING: Tomatillo and ground cherry seedlings are planted into bales exactly as described for tomatoes (see next page). They are frost-sensitive, so be sure to wait until nighttime temperatures are above 32°F.

Tomatoes

Gardeners have access to an incredible range of tomato varieties these days. Garden centers seem to stock a wider selection every year, seed catalogs provide hundreds more, and access to seed-saving and seed-sharing organizations such as the Seed Savers Exchange expand the number well into the thousands. The more direct sun your bale receives, the more success you'll have with larger-fruited varieties; cherry tomatoes are the best bet for lesser sun exposure. It's also important to know whether a variety is determinate or indeterminate (see page 75), so that you can offer it the right support.

In my trials, tomatoes grown in straw bales grew at least as well as those grown in the ground or in a container. The lack of soil-borne diseases in straw bales is a big advantage; disease-prone tomato varieties that may have struggled in the ground do better in straw bales.

DENSITY: With the exception of the dwarfs (see page 75), tomatoes are such heavy feeders and vigorous growers that I recommend no more than two plants per bale.

PLANTING: Wait to plant tomatoes until the threat of night-time frost is past. Visually divide the bale in half, and dig a depression into the straw bale in the middle of each half; ensure that each depression is deep enough so that the tomato stem can be buried up to its first true leaves. Roots will develop along any part of the tomato stem that is beneath the surface. Remove the tomato seedling from the container, retaining as much of the soil around the root ball as possible, and insert it into the bale. Fill in around the root ball and stem with planting medium, and gently tamp it down. Mulch the area with shredded leaves or grass clippings to minimize moisture loss from the surface. Gently water the area around the base of the transplant.

Refer to pages 33–39 for ideas on providing support.

tomato seedlings

Types of Tomatoes

Indeterminate: Indeterminate tomato plants grow upward and outward infinitely, flowering and fruiting continually until killed by frost or disease or pruned. Many popular hybrid varieties, such as Better Boy and Sun Gold, and most heirloom types, like Cherokee Purple and Brandywine, are indeterminate. Tall stakes or tomato cages (at least 6 feet high) are used to support this type of tomato.

Determinate: There are far fewer determinate varieties available to choose from, but some are well known, such as Celebrity, Roma, and Taxi. Determinate tomato varieties are genetically coded to be self-limiting in height, width, and yield. Typically they grow to 3 to 4 feet tall and 2 to 3 feet wide, set flowers at the branch tips, and ripen a heavy yield of tomatoes in a fairly compact time frame. Though they can be grown unsupported, they can still sprawl considerably. Cone-shaped tomato cages work well.

Dwarf: This tomato type is the least known, but recent breeding is expanding the possibilities. Older Dwarfs are represented by Dwarf Champion, and newer releases are Lime Green Salad, Rosella Purple, and Dwarf Sweet Sue. They can provide the same array of color, size, and flavor as indeterminate types but will be easier to control. They exhibit the vertical expansion of the determinate varieties but an all-season fruiting habit of the indeterminate types. Dwarf tomatoes can be controlled in the same manner as determinate tomatoes.

CHAPTER SEVEN

PROBLEM SOLVING

Each garden provides opportunities to solve the inevitable unexpected problems that arise from weather, diseases, or critters. Often, careful observation of the plants provides plenty of hints for suggested remedial actions.

It is important to remember that every garden will experience dilemmas and challenges. They are not a reflection of the skill of the gardeners, but rather of the fickle nature of growing plants, place to place and season to season. The main point is to identify issues quickly, and either resolve them if possible, or learn what needs to be done differently next season.

FEEDING AND WATERING

Issues that arise from insufficient watering will show up when the plants are large and beginning to set and/or mature their crops). Thirsty plants tell you about their water shortage by wilting. Since bales can't be overwatered, err on the side of too much, rather than too little, watering. If watering doesn't alleviate the wilting, a disease may be the culprit (see pages 78–79).

Frequent watering will leach fertilizers away quickly, leaving the roots in need of nutrition. If the formerly lush, deep green plants emerging from the bales become faded, increase the feeding frequency. Since bales provide very little nutrition themselves, be sure to use balanced fertilizers (either inorganic or organic), and be aware of any particular special nutritional needs for the crops you are growing.

Too Much Foliage, Not Enough Fruit

Very vigorous, lush plants with few developing vegetables could indicate either a lack of nutritional balance for the plants in that particular bale, a lack of insect pollinators, or simply temporarily poor conditions for the given crop to set fruit.

Crops that don't require cross-pollination, such as those in the tomato or legume families, should produce lots of blossoms. If the plant has a lot of leaves but few flowers, you may be overfeeding the bale with nitrogen. If flowers are adequate to plentiful, but they are dropping off without setting fruit, the plant may be unhappy with the temperature or humidity levels.

Over the course of the season the conditions will likely become favorable, so all you need is a little patience.

For plants that require pollination, which includes vining crops such as melons, cucumbers, and squash, flower-visiting insects are a must. If you are short of bees, be sure to have other bee-attracting crops such as flowers and herbs nearby.

Wilting or Fading Plants

One significant advantage of growing plants in straw bales is the ability to plant in a medium that is devoid of soil-borne diseases. For example, I've found that some sensitive heirloom tomatoes that are vulnerable to disease when grown in my garden are far more successful in bales.

Blossom End Rot

If young tomatoes and peppers start to develop dark spots on the blossom end, the problem isn't a disease, but a physiological issue related to the movement of calcium out of the developing fruit, brought about by insufficient or uneven watering. Although blossom end rot should be less of an issue in straw bale gardening than in traditional in-ground gardens, sudden changes in the weather (rainfall or temperature) could initiate the problem. Since calcium is so critical to healthy fruit formation, ensure that your balanced fertilizer of choice lists it as an ingredient. To ensure that young fruit-laden plants don't visibly wilt, provide sufficient water at the base of the plant, especially during hot spells.

This doesn't mean that it is impossible for bale-grown plants to become diseased. Some chewing insects carry diseases, and fungal spores can blow in from nearby gardens or weeds. Plant diseases can also be introduced via infected seeds or transplants.

If disease hits some of your bale-grown plants, spend some time trying to identify the problem. There is a treasure of information about plant diseases on the Internet (see References, page 86, for a few good sites). Contact your local agricultural extension service for advice. In most cases, diseased plants are best removed and destroyed. Since many diseases travel into the roots of the plant, be sure to note which bales had problem plants, remove the bale material from the garden, and destroy it by burning or relocating to an area where it won't get mistakenly used or composed.

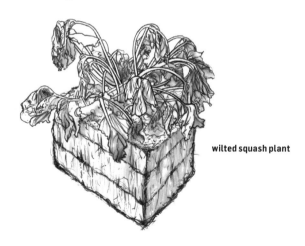

wilted squash plant

PESTS AND CRITTERS

THE MOIST, WARM, SHADED HABITAT a straw bale creates is an irresistible combination for many critters. Fortunately, visiting your bales frequently to water, fertilize, and harvest will keep many critters away. Also, bales placed in areas with a lot of human activity, such as decks and yards, are less likely than isolated bales to receive unwanted visitors. There are always exceptions, however.

Some gardeners have reported that snakes use their bales for nesting or protection. Heavily seeded bales may attract mice, which would attract the snakes. Be observant when working around your bales in case a snake takes an interest in your garden. If you live in an area with high snake populations, use a long pole to carefully poke around the bottom of the bales before approaching them, just to be sure there are no surprises awaiting you.

Any critter that pays attention to in-ground or container gardens — such as deer, squirrels, or birds — could also provide trouble for your bale garden. Physical barriers, such as fences or cages, always work best to deter these pests. Motion-activated sprinklers work really well to keep deer away. Feeders and water sources placed elsewhere on your property may draw birds and squirrels away from your garden.

The rough, dry surface of straw bales and elevation from the ground would seem to deter slugs, but these pests do sometimes find their way to the top of the bale. To create a surface that slugs will not cross, apply diatomaceous earth or sharp gravel around the base of plants. You can also place a shallow pan of beer at the base of the bale; the slugs will be lured into it and drown.

All of the usual insect pests that bother gardeners in your area will be drawn to your bale-grown plants, so be sure to have various tactics ready to deal with the inevitable attacks. To spray or not to spray, as well as what to spray, is a very individual and often philosophical decision for each gardener. Most pests, such as tomato hornworms, stink bugs, and Japanese beetles, are easy to see and can be removed through handpicking.

More challenging are tiny, plentiful, or relatively voracious pests such as tomato fruit worms, Colorado potato and cucumber beetles, aphids, cabbage loopers, whiteflies, and flea beetles. This is where your decisions of whether to dust and/or spray and, if so, what type of agent to use will be most important. A light, floating row cover draped over the bale can provide a useful physical barrier against insect attacks.

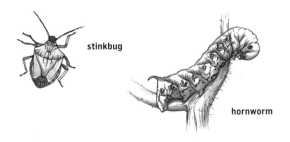

stinkbug

hornworm

CHAPTER EIGHT

WHAT REMAINS

It was remarkable to discover the fate of my bales as I did my end-of-the-season garden cleanup. I could recall unloading the bales from my truck and hauling them into position — tight, tidy bundles of stiff, dry straw. After a season of being watered and fed, weathering the elements, and hosting hungry roots and migrating worms, the bales were razed.

When one considers the expense of compost (either homemade or purchased), or bagged potting mixes, the inherent value in the remains of the bales should bring smiles to the faces of all gardeners.

Once the harvest was complete, any hopes I had of relocating the bales as units vanished with my very first attempt. The two fiber cords that were wrapped around the bales and provided the initial integrity slipped right off. It was easy to drive a shovel into the bale and break it into pieces. What I found inside was fluffy, beautiful black organic matter. Over the course of the season, that hard, stiff straw had been converted into compost-like material that I shoveled into my wheelbarrow and spread onto my garden rows to provide a nice bed for next season's efforts.

When considering what to do with your used bales, it is important to keep track of what you grew in them and whether any of those plants developed diseases. Bales used for tomatoes, peppers, or cucumbers that became infected with various wilts should not be used to provide mulch or compost for those types of plants in the following season. Bales that grew healthy plants can be used to fill frames or pots next season; it is unlikely that they can be used as freestanding bales for a second time.

If you positioned your bales on a deck or patio, you will need a wheelbarrow or large container and a shovel in order to remove them. In all likelihood, the bales will not be solid enough to simply lift and transfer, but the supporting strings should slip off easily and the crumbly, dark, loamy material beneath the dry outer straw layer is easy to dump into the wheelbarrow.

If you had your bales positioned in a garden, simply remove the strings, knock the bales apart with a shovel, and spread the remains around the garden to enrich the soil and improve the structure. You can also transfer the remains to a wheelbarrow and pile it up for use the following year as a mulch, compost, or filler for containers.

If you went through the expense and effort of making containing structures for the bales, you have a head start on some easy possibilities for next season. The broken-down bales will be perfect for crops such as potatoes, carrots, onions, beets, and garlic — all of which love growing in a fluffy, rock-free

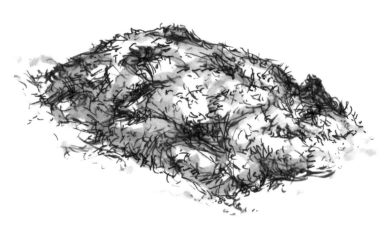

BALES THAT DO THEIR WORK for a full gardening season typically break down completely, leaving useful mulch for next year's garden.

substrate. The one caution is to make sure that the initial plants in those bales were free of diseases. You may need to add a bit of organic matter or planting medium to the top in areas where there is collapse or structural loss.

No matter where you positioned the bales or what you grew in them, bale remains are valuable for use in future gardens, so be sure to take advantage of this ready-made organic treasure.

REFERENCES

"Accessible Gardening: Hay Bale Gardening." Center for Excellence in Disabilities, West Virginia University. *http://greenthumbs.cedwvu.org/factsheets/hay-bale.php*

Antongiovanni, M., and C. Sargentini. "Variability in Chemical Composition of Straws," *Options Méditerranéenes: Série A. Séminaires Méditerranéens*, n. 16 (1991): 49–53. *http://om.ciheam.org/om/pdf/a16/91605044.pdf*

Card, Adrian, David Whiting, Carl Wilson, and Jean Reeder. "Organic Fertilizers." *CMG GardenNotes* #234, Colorado State University Extension, 2014. *www.ext.colostate.edu/mg/gardennotes/234.html*

Daily, Cado. "Gardening in Straw Bales." University of Arizona Cooperative Extension, 2013. *http://cals.arizona.edu/cochise/waterwise/pdf/GardeningStrawbalegardens_6-13.pdf*

Desta, Kefyalew Girma, and Marianne Ophardt. "Straw Bale Gardening." Fact Sheet FS109E, Washington State University Extension, 2013. *http://cru.cahe.wsu.edu/CEPublications/FS109E/FS109E.pdf*

Douglas, Ellen. "How to Grow Strawberries in Hay Bales." SFGate Home Guide. *http://homeguides.sfgate.com/grow-strawberries-hay-bales-30457.html*

Iannotti, Marie. "What is a Soilless Potting Mix?" About.com. *http://gardening.about.com/od/seedsavin1/a/Potting_Mix.htm*

Jolly, Nicole Cotroneo. "How to Build a Straw Bale Garden." *Modern Farmer*, July 16, 2013. *http://modernfarmer.com/2013/07/straw-bale-gardening*

Karsten, Joel. *Straw Bale Gardening.* Cool Springs Press, 2013.

Michaels, Kerry. "The Pros and Cons of Straw Bale Gardening." About.com. *http://containergardening.about.com/od/vegetablesandherbs/qt/The -Pros-And-Cons-Of-Straw-Bale-Gardening.htm*

Nagel, David, Wayne Porter, and Stanley Wise. "Growing in the Bale." Information Sheet 1678, Mississippi State University Extension Service, 2005. *http://msucares.com/pubs/infosheets/is1678.pdf*

Johnston County, NC Forums. 4042.com. *http://forums.4042.com* Home of the former Straw Bale Gardening Forum

Ryczkowski, Angela. "How to Grow Sweet Potatoes in Straw Bales." SFGate Home Guide. *http://homeguides.sfgate.com/grow-sweet-potatoes- straw-bales-80093.html*

Trimble, Kelly Smith. "A Raised Bed Twist: Straw Bale Gardening." HGTV Gardens. *www.hgtvgardens.comraised-gardenraised-bed-with-a-twist -straw-bale-gardening*

Metric Conversion Charts

Approximate Equivalent by Volume

U.S.	METRIC
¼ cup	60 milliliters
½ cup	120 milliliters
¾ cup	175 milliliters
1 cup	230 milliliters
1½ cups	360 milliliters
2 cups	460 milliliters
3 cups	700 milliliters

Temperature

TO CONVERT	TO	
Fahrenheit	Celsius	subtract 32 from Fahrenheit temperature, multiply by 5, then divide by 9

Approximate Equivalent by Length

U.S.	METRIC	U.S.	METRIC
½ inch	1.27 centimeters	12 inches/1 foot	30.48 centimeters
¾ inch	1.91 centimeters	2 feet	0.61 meters
1 inch	2.54 centimeters	3 feet	0.91 meters
1 ½ inch	3.81 centimeters	4 feet	1.22 meters
2 inches	5.08 centimeters	5 feet	1.52 meters
3 inches	7.62 centimeters	6 feet	1.83 meters
4 inches	10.16 centimeters	7 feet	2.13 meters
5 inches	12.70 centimeters	8 feet	2.44 meters
6 inches	15.24 centimeters		

INDEX

Page numbers in *italic* indicate illustrations.

OTHER STOREY BOOKS YOU WILL ENJOY

Epic Tomatoes by Craig LeHoullier
Grow your best tomatoes with this fascinating and beautiful guide by expert gardener Craig LeHoullier. Packed with insights and enthralling photography, *Epic Tomatoes* explains everything a tomato enthusiast needs to know about growing more than 200 varieties of hybrid and heirloom tomatoes.
256 pages. Paper. ISBN 978-1-61212-208-3.
Hardcover. ISBN 978-1-61212-464-3.

Carrots Love Tomatoes by Louise Riotte
This classic companion planting guide shows how to use plants' natural partnerships to produce bigger and better harvests.
224 pages. Paper. ISBN 978-1-58017-027-7.

Container Theme Gardens by Nancy J. Ondra
Enjoy gorgeous container plantings with 42 planting combinations, each using five specially matched plants. With themes for every taste and setting from Hummingbird Haven and Winter Wonders to Pond in a Pot and Bursting with Berries, you'll find the perfect mix for your style!
272 pages. Paper. ISBN 978-1-61212-398-1.

Starter Vegetable Gardens by Barbara Pleasant
Start small and grow big with this great resource for beginning vegetable gardeners offering 24 no-fail plans for small organic gardens.
180 pages. Paper. ISBN 978-1-60342-529-2.

The Vegetable Gardener's Container Bible by Edward C. Smith
Veteran gardener Edward C. Smith presents detailed, illustrated advice on how to choose the right plants for a small-space container garden and care for them throughout the season.
264 pages. Paper. ISBN 978-1-60342-975-7.

These and other books from Storey Publishing are available wherever quality books are sold or by calling 1-800-441-5700.
Visit us at *www.storey.com* or sign up for our newsletter at *www.storey.com/signup*.